MOVIE MAGIC
MOTION CAPTURE

BY SARA GREEN

BELLWETHER MEDIA • MINNEAPOLIS, MN

Blastoff! Discovery launches
a new mission: reading to learn.
Filled with facts and features, each
book offers you an exciting new
world to explore!

This edition first published in 2020 by Bellwether Media, Inc.

No part of this publication may be reproduced in whole or in
part without written permission of the publisher.
For information regarding permission, write to
Bellwether Media, Inc., Attention: Permissions Department,
6012 Blue Circle Drive, Minnetonka, MN 55343.

Library of Congress Cataloging-in-Publication Data

Names: Green, Sara, 1964- author.
Title: Motion Capture / by Sara Green.
Description: Minneapolis, MN : Bellwether Media, Inc., 2020.
    | Series: Blastoff! Discovery. Movie Magic | Audience:
    Ages: 7 to 13. | Audience: Grades: 3 through 8. | Includes
    bibliographical references and index.
Identifiers: LCCN 2019000935 (print) | LCCN 2019013018
    (ebook) | ISBN 9781618915849 (ebook) | ISBN
    9781644870433 (hardcover : alk. paper)
Subjects: LCSH: Computer animation–Juvenile literature. |
    Human locomotion–Computer simulation–Juvenile literature.
    | Motion–Computer simulation–Juvenile literature.
Classification: LCC TR897.7 (ebook) | LCC TR897.7 .G735
    2020 (print) | DDC 776/.6–dc23
LC record available at https://lccn.loc.gov/2019000935

Editor: Betsy Rathburn   Designer: Brittany McIntosh

Printed in the United States of America, North Mankato, MN.

TABLE OF CONTENTS

APES IN CHARGE!

Apes charge through a forest! They carry spears and other weapons. These apes look real. But human actors played them! The 2014 film *Dawn of the Planet of the Apes* used motion capture to **transform** actors into apes.

DAWN OF THE PLANET OF THE APES

When the actors arrived on **set**, they were not wearing ape costumes. They wore tight bodysuits covered with markers called **sensors**. The actors also wore motion-capture headsets. Sensors dotted their faces.

APE WALK

Many of the actors playing apes wore arm extensions. This helped them walk on their hands and feet!

The actors moved like apes to play their roles. Dozens of special cameras captured their movements. Small cameras were also attached to their headsets. The cameras used the sensors to capture the actors' facial expressions. This information was stored in a computer program that creates **CGI**.

SENSORS

Animators used special software to design the apes. The animators made the apes' gestures and expressions look human. On screen, the apes do not appear animated. They look real!

WHAT IS MOTION CAPTURE?

Motion capture, or mocap, is a technology that matches human movement to CGI characters. Actors wear sensors that record their movements. This information is used to create CGI characters that move like real people.

Mocap markers can capture almost any movement, large or small. Actors smile, crawl, and leap on set. CGI characters follow their motions exactly! Mocap allows actors to avoid hours of makeup. They can also avoid risky situations. The CGI characters face the dangers instead!

BEHIND THE SCENES OF *TARZAN*

LED MARKER

OPTICAL MOTION CAPTURE IN
ALITA: BATTLE ANGEL

Motion capture can be done in different ways. Filmmakers often use **optical** mocap. Actors wear tight-fitting suits covered with sensors. Special cameras record light from the markers as the actors move. Some markers reflect light. They look like bulbs. Other markers, like LED lights, **emit** light.

The cameras send information about the lights' locations to a computer. Filmmakers use software to attach CGI characters to these points of light. This way, the characters move just like the actors!

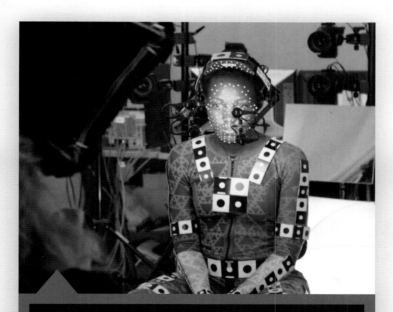

MECHANICAL MOTION CAPTURE

Some filmmakers use mechanical motion capture. Actors wear a frame lined with sensors over their clothes. The sensors send information to a computer as the actors move.

HISTORY OF MOTION CAPTURE

The history of motion capture starts with early animation. Animators wanted to make character movements look real. But early cartoon characters often looked jerky and stiff.

A filmmaker named Max Fleischer helped solve this problem. In the 1910s, he invented an animation tool called the **rotoscope**. Max filmed actors moving. Then he used the **footage** to create **cel animation**. Actors' movements were traced onto clear plastic. The animated characters matched their movements!

ROTOSCOPE

MOTION CAPTURE PIONEER

Name: Max Fleischer
Born: July 19, 1883, in Krakow, Poland
Known For: Animator and inventor who created the rotoscope and brought characters such as Betty Boop, Popeye, and Superman to life

POPEYE

The rotoscope soon became a popular animation tool. Walt Disney used it to make many of his early films. The rotoscope helped bring characters to life in early Disney movies. Some favorites are *Snow White and the Seven Dwarfs* and *Pinocchio*!

Over time, many other animators have used the rotoscope to create lifelike characters in films, video games, and music videos. A rotoscope was even used to make the glowing lightsabers in the 1977 film *Star Wars: Episode IV — A New Hope*!

EARLY MOCAP

Director Ralph Bakshi used rotoscoping to make the characters in the 1978 animated film *The Lord of the Rings*.

BEHIND THE SCENES OF
ALICE IN WONDERLAND

MOTION CAPTURE
RESEARCH

Rotoscoping was the **forerunner** to motion capture. Computer use began to grow in the 1970s. The new technology led to motion capture. Mocap first started as a research tool. Scientists used it to study human movement. It helped them see how knees and other body parts move.

By the mid-1990s, motion capture had moved into the world of entertainment. Video game makers began using motion capture to make characters that looked real.

REALISTIC ROBOTS

The 1994 game *The Rise of the Robots* was the first video game created with motion capture.

Motion capture was introduced to filmmaking in the 1990s. During this time, mocap was done in special **studios** away from movie sets and the other actors.

Motion capture was used for **stunts** for the 1995 film *Batman Forever*. It also helped make characters appear to fall off a ship in the 1997 film *Titanic*. A character named Jar Jar Binks stars in the 1999 film *Star Wars: Episode I — The Phantom Menace*. Motion capture helped bring him to life, too!

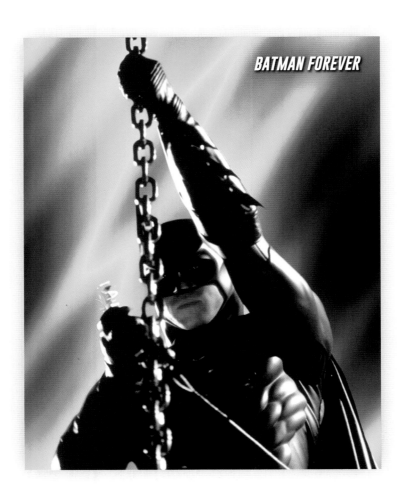

BATMAN FOREVER

EYES ON JAR JAR

Actor Ahmed Best provided the motion capture and voice for Jar Jar Binks. Best wore a hat that looked like Jar Jar's head during motion capture sessions. It helped other actors focus on Jar Jar's eyes instead of Ahmed's eyes!

BEHIND THE SCENES OF
STAR WARS: EPISODE I –
THE PHANTOM MENACE

MASTERING MOCAP

Motion capture technology continued improving. In 2002, the film *The Lord of the Rings: The Two Towers* was released. It includes a character named Gollum. Actor Andy Serkis provided the motion capture and voice.

Andy first shot his **scenes** on set with other actors. His costume made it easy for filmmakers to create a CGI version of his character. Later, Andy repeated his performance on a mocap set. His performance helped animators get the character's movements right. Andy's motion capture performance was groundbreaking. Gollum's lifelike appearance amazed audiences!

GOLLUM

MODERN MOTION CAPTURE MASTER

Name: Andy Serkis
Born: April 20, 1964, in Ruislip, England
Known For: Actor whose motion capture performance as Gollum in the Lord of the Rings film series (2001-2003) broke new ground for the technology, and who went on to mocap performances in the Planet of the Apes film series (2011-2017), *The Force Awakens* (2015), and many others
Awards: Many awards, including two Screen Actors Guild Awards for his work in *The Lord of the Rings: The Return of the King* and *Black Panther*

ANDY SERKIS IN *DAWN OF THE PLANET OF THE APES*

Motion capture took another step forward in the 2000s. *Sinbad: Beyond the Veil of Mists* became the first full-length film made entirely using motion capture.

The 2004 film *The Polar Express* was the first CGI film to use both mocap and facial capture. Actor Tom Hanks played many of the film's characters. He wore sensors that helped animators match the characters' facial expressions to his. The movie led to many future mocap films!

THE POLAR EXPRESS

MOCAP LINGO

A motion capture studio is also known as a motion capture volume in the filmmaking world.

SINBAD: BEYOND THE VEIL OF MISTS

BEHIND THE SCENES OF
AVATAR

Director James Cameron improved facial capture for the 2009 film *Avatar*. The story features aliens who live on a faraway moon. The actors playing the aliens performed motion capture in front of dozens of cameras.

Tiny cameras mounted to caps captured the actors' facial expressions. Animators used the recordings to create the movie's aliens. The characters have humanlike blinks, smiles, and frowns. Motion capture helped make *Avatar* an award-winning hit!

HORSING AROUND

Motion capture helped make the direhorses in *Avatar* look real. Live horses played the roles. They wore mocap sensors on their bodies as the actors rode them on set!

MOTION CAPTURE IN THE MOVIES

Movie: *Ready Player One*

Year: 2018

Famous For: Many characters and even some props created using motion capture, including a DeLorean car that was made by putting mocap sensors on a real-life car

Awards: Nominated for many awards, including the Academy Award for Best Visual Effects

Motion capture has helped create many other memorable film characters. Actor Benedict Cumberbatch played the dragon Smaug in the 2013 film *The Hobbit: The Desolation of Smaug.* He performed the role in mocap gear. Motion capture also made the film's orcs and goblins look real.

Motion capture was also used to develop important characters in the Avengers film series. Mocap helped Thanos, Ultron, and the Incredible Hulk appear lifelike on screen.

BEHIND THE SCENES OF *THE HOBBIT: THE DESOLATION OF SMAUG*

ENDLESS POSSIBILITIES!

Motion capture technology continues to improve. **Machine learning** is helping filmmakers explore markerless motion capture. Computers can learn to create face and body movements without sensors or directions from people. Instead, the computers can take information directly from the cameras. Then they create characters while the actors are performing!

Advances in motion capture lead to even more lifelike movies. Recent films such as *Dumbo* and *The Lion King* used motion capture to bring cartoon animals to life!

DUMBO

MARKERLESS
MOTION CAPTURE

GLOSSARY

animated—made up of images that look as though they are moving

animators—artists who draw or use computers to create animations

cel animation—a type of animation in which characters and other details are drawn on clear plastic sheets and moved across a fixed background

CGI—artwork created by computers; CGI stands for computer-generated imagery.

director—a person who controls the making of a movie

emit—to give off or send out

footage—filmed material made for movies or television

forerunner—something that came before something else

machine learning—the ability of computers to learn new information on their own

optical—related to visible light; optical motion capture involves cameras picking up light from sensors.

rotoscope—a device used by animators to trace actors' movements onto film

scenes—the action in single places and times in films or plays

sensors—small devices worn by actors to capture motion

set—the place where a movie is made

software—computer programs that do specific tasks; motion capture software uses actors' movements to create CGI characters.

studios—places where movies are filmed

stunts—dangerous or risky acts in movies

transform—to change

TO LEARN MORE

AT THE LIBRARY

Gregory, Joshua. *Careers in Virtual Reality Technology*. Ann Arbor, Mich.: Cherry Lake Publishing, 2019.

Horn, Geoffrey M. *Movie Animation*. Milwaukee, Wisc.: Gareth Stevens Publishing, 2007.

Wood, John. *Moviemaking Technology: 4D, Motion Capture, and More*. New York, N.Y.: Gareth Stevens Publishing, 2019.

ON THE WEB

FACTSURFER

Factsurfer.com gives you a safe, fun way to find more information.

1. Go to www.factsurfer.com.

2. Enter "motion capture" into the search box and click 🔍.

3. Select your book cover to see a list of related web sites.

INDEX

The images in this book are reproduced through the courtesy of: Album/ Alamy, front cover; Moviestore collection Ltd/ Alamy, pp. 4-5, 25; Collection Christophel/ Alamy, pp. 6, 20, 21; Photo 12/ Alamy, pp. 6-7, 9 (top), 11, 19 (top); PictureLux/ The Hollywood Archive/ Alamy, p. 8; AF archive/ Alamy, p. 9 (bottom); Twentieth Century Fox Film Corp/ Everett Collection, p. 10 (top, bottom); Max Fleischer/ Wikipedia, p. 12; CPL Archives/ Everett Collection, p. 13 (top); Everett Collection, p. 13 (bottom); United Artists/ Everett Collection p. 14; RKO Radio Pictures/ Photofest Digital, p. 15 (top, bottom); 615 collection/ Alamy, p. 16; Wikipedia, p. 17; Warner Brothers/ Photofest Digital, p. 18; Lucasfilm Ltd./ 20th Century Fox/ Photofest Digital, p. 19 (bottom); Warner Brothers/ Everett Collection, p. 22; Trimark Pictures/ Photofest Digital, p. 23; 20th Century Fox/ Everett Collection, p. 24 (top); Twentieth Century-Fox Film Corporation/ Photofest Digital, p. 24 (bottom); Warner Bros. Pictures/ Everett Collection, p. 26; Warner Bros./ Everett Collection, p. 27 (top); TCD/ Prod.DB/ Alamy, p. 27 (bottom); Lifestyle pictures/ Alamy, p. 28; age fotostock/ Alamy, p. 29.